EYE TWISTERS

BOGGLE, BAFFLE AND BLOW YOUR MIND!

This is a Carlton book

Text, design and illustration copyright
© 2014 Carlton Books Limited

Author and Editor: Anna Bowles
Jacket Designer: Jake da'Costa
Designer: Rebecca Wright
Production: Ena Matagic

Published in 2013 by Carlton Books Limited
An imprint of the Carlton Publishing Group
20 Mortimer Street, London W1T 3JW

10 9 8 7 6 5 4 3 2 1

A catalogue record for this book is available from the British
Library.

ISBN: 978-1-78312-033-8
Printed in Dongguan, China

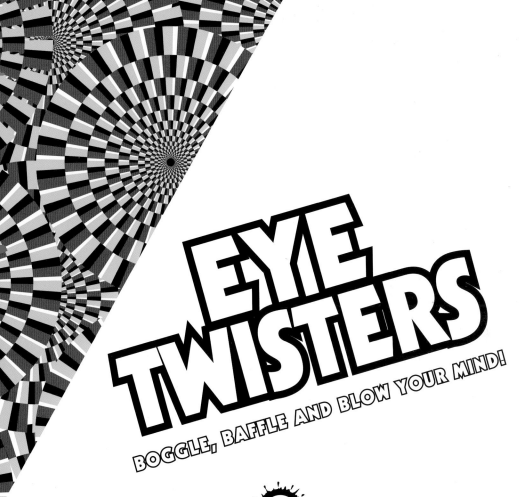

EYE TWISTERS

BOGGLE, BAFFLE AND BLOW YOUR MIND!

CARLTON
KiDS

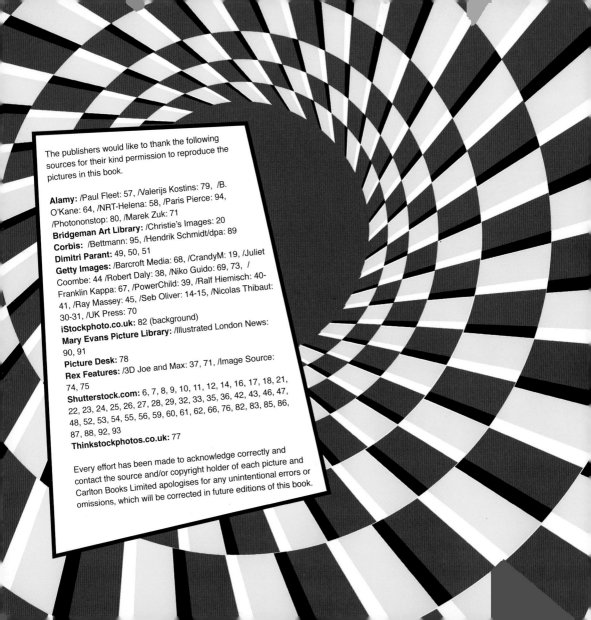

The publishers would like to thank the following sources for their kind permission to reproduce the pictures in this book.

Alamy: /Paul Fleet: 57, /Valerijs Kostins: 79, /B. O'Kane: 64, /NRT-Helena: 58, /Paris Pierce: 94, /Photononstop: 80, /Marek Zuk: 71
Bridgeman Art Library: /Christie's Images: 20
Corbis: /Bettmann: 95, /Hendrik Schmidt/dpa: 89
Dimitri Parant: 49, 50, 51
Getty Images: /Barcroft Media: 68, /CrandyM: 19, /Juliet Coombe: 44 /Robert Daly: 38, /Niko Guido: 69, 73, / Franklin Kappa: 67, /PowerChild: 39, /Ralf Hiemisch: 40-41, /Ray Massey: 45, /Seb Oliver: 14-15, /Nicolas Thibaut: 30-31, /UK Press: 70
iStockphoto.co.uk: 82 (background)
Mary Evans Picture Library: /Illustrated London News: 90, 91
Picture Desk: 78
Rex Features: /3D Joe and Max: 37, 71, /Image Source: 74, 75
Shutterstock.com: 6, 7, 8, 9, 10, 11, 12, 14, 16, 17, 18, 21, 22, 23, 24, 25, 26, 27, 28, 29, 32, 33, 35, 36, 42, 43, 46, 47, 48, 52, 53, 54, 55, 56, 59, 60, 61, 62, 66, 76, 82, 83, 85, 86, 87, 88, 92, 93
Thinkstockphotos.co.uk: 77

Every effort has been made to acknowledge correctly and contact the source and/or copyright holder of each picture and Carlton Books Limited apologises for any unintentional errors or omissions, which will be corrected in future editions of this book.

OPTICAL ILLUSIONS...

What you see is not quite what you get! This book is full of pulsing patterns, twisting twirls and impossible shapes that will bend your eyes upside out and downside in, leaving you feeling thoroughly boggled. There are also some good tricks for you to try at home.

Enjoy, and don't forget to blink!

IMPOSSIBLE CUBE

Sometimes you can draw an object that would be impossible to make in three dimensions. Can you draw a cube like this one?

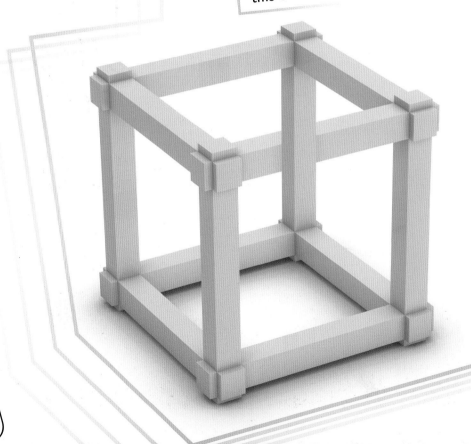

SCINTILLATING GRID

Look for the dots – but not too
hard, or they'll vanish!

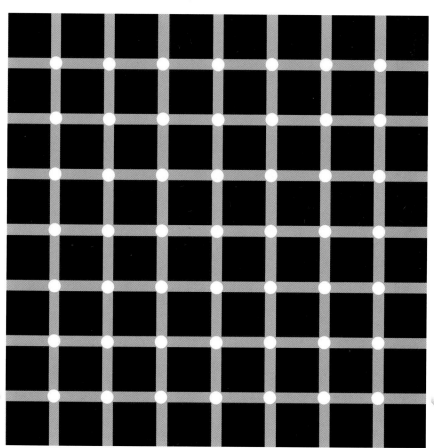

INTERLOCKING IMPOSSIBILITIES

Have the cubes from page 6 been breeding?

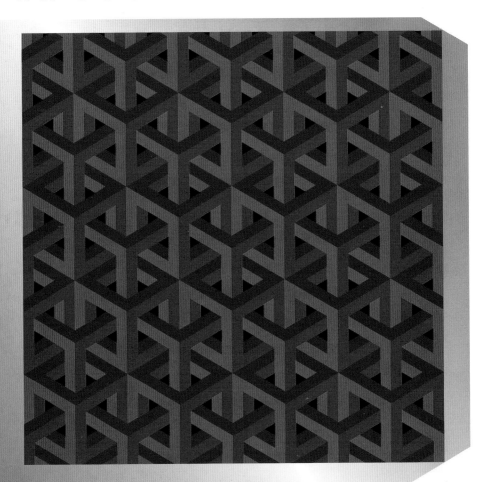

PULSATING PURPLE

Is this a crumpled paper napkin, or pulsating waves of colour?

CONVEX OR CONCAVE?

Are you looking at the top of a pyramid, or peering down a tunnel?

CORNER QUANDARY

Are these cubes bulging out at you, or bending in? Can they do both?

BOGUS BULGE

The gradually changing shapes mimic a flat piece of paper that bulges. So a bulge is what you see!

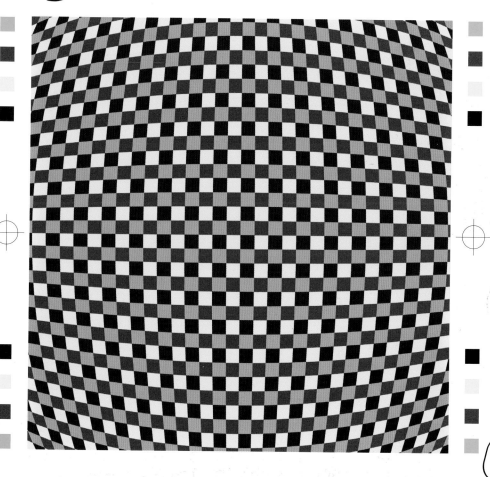

TRY THIS ONE AT HOME!

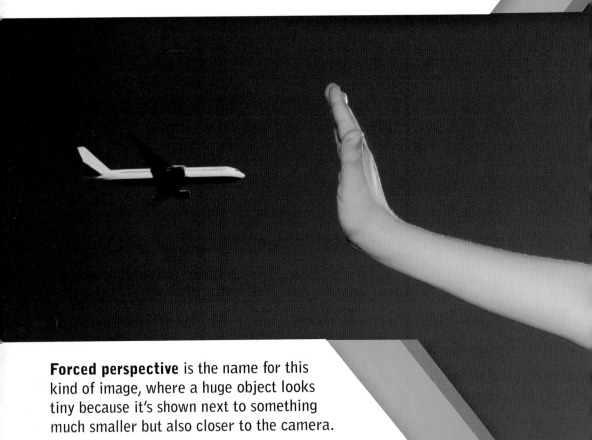

Forced perspective is the name for this kind of image, where a huge object looks tiny because it's shown next to something much smaller but also closer to the camera.

Can you set up your own photo like this one in your back garden or school playground?

ETERNAL TURNING

The wheels spin slowly and endlessly - until you look directly at one of them. Then that one stops!

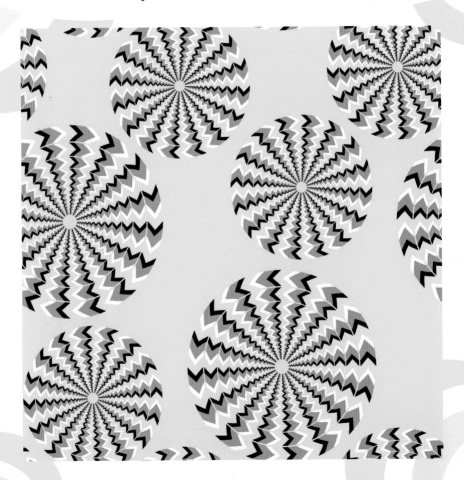

GIRLS OR GLASS?

In this classic illusion, do you see a fancy glass goblet, or two faces about to kiss?

TWITCHING TREE

Are these leaves hanging motionless on a hot day, or waving in a cool breeze?

WHICH WINDOWS?

This is a very strange block of flats. Are those windows, skylights or holes in the floor?

FRUIT FOOL?

This is an ordinary picture of a basket of fruit... until you turn it upside down.

INWARDS OR OUTWARDS?

Multiple waterfalls of chocolate sliding into infinity, or a mud pie explosion – which is it?

SPOT THE PETAL

Can you see petal shapes in this amazing image? Or are there just black and white squares?

COUNT THE CUBES

Can you pick out seven big cubes in this picture? Some of them are only partly visible.

SEEING STARS

Stare at this circling illusion and the outer stars turn clockwise while the inner ones go the other way!

DICING WITH DIMENSIONS

This cube of dice is a more complex version of the illusion on page 8. Can you draw this one too?

SQUARING THE CIRCLE

Are these squares and rectangles flat or domed?

FLOWER BURSTS

Sit back and watch the flowers
grow before your very eyes!

STATIONARY SHUFFLE

It's the dancers from page 10 again. Are they lying down for a rest, or wriggling across the sand?

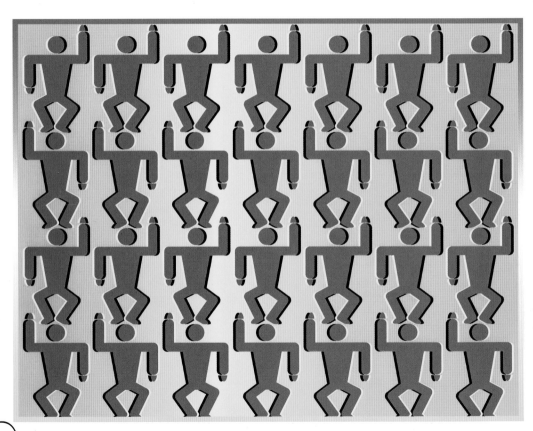

TRY
THIS
ONE
AT
HOME!

You don't need to visit the Leaning Tower of Pisa to set up a picture like this – try it with a large tree.

STREET SEEN?

Can you spot which parts of this street scene are real, and which are painted on a blank wall?

SUN SHOCK

The waves coming out of the sun here seem to almost jerk in and out as your eye expects to see one thing but actually sees another, and quickly adjusts.

LINE UP THE LINES

Are the lines between the squares straight or
bendy? Your ruler may disagree with your eyes!

SKY TEASER

Can you guess what this is?
The answer is below.

It's a photo of a glass-windowed skyscraper reflecting the sky, set against a different photo of the sky.

TWO WAYS AT ONCE

This circling image seems to move in jerks.
Is the motion clockwise or anticlockwise?

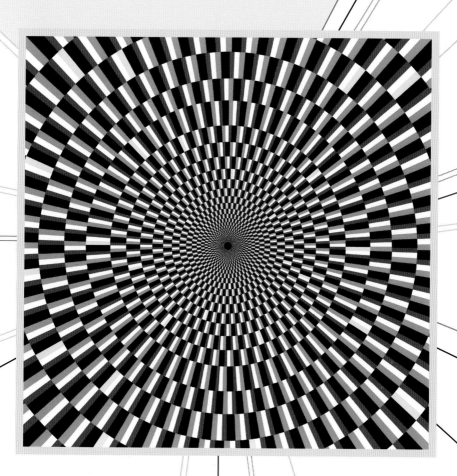

CHECKERBOARD WARP

Can you follow an alternating series of black and white squares from one side of the page to the other without blinking?

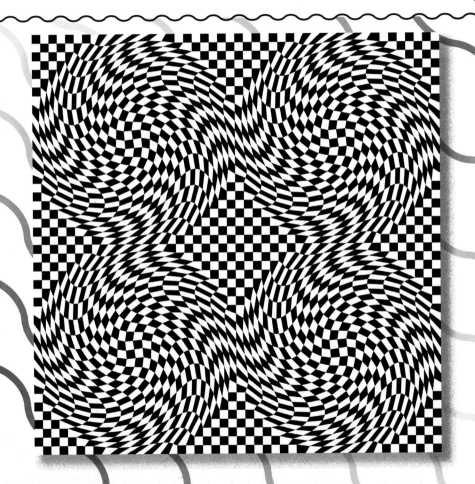

FLOORED!

This clever painting makes it appear that a hole in the room's floor goes through to a similar room below.

TRY THIS ONE AT HOME!

Here's another one you can reproduce yourself. Get your friend to stand far away from you, hold up your hand and take a picture of the result.

RHOMBUSES, REALLY

It's easy to see this image as three-dimensional cubes, but can you see it as two-dimensional rhombuses? (A rhombus is a four-sided shape where all sides have equal length.)

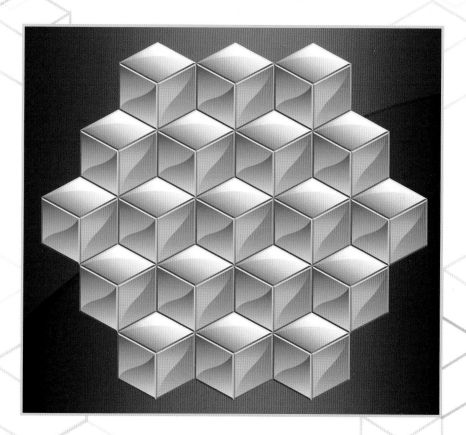

RAINBOW RAYS

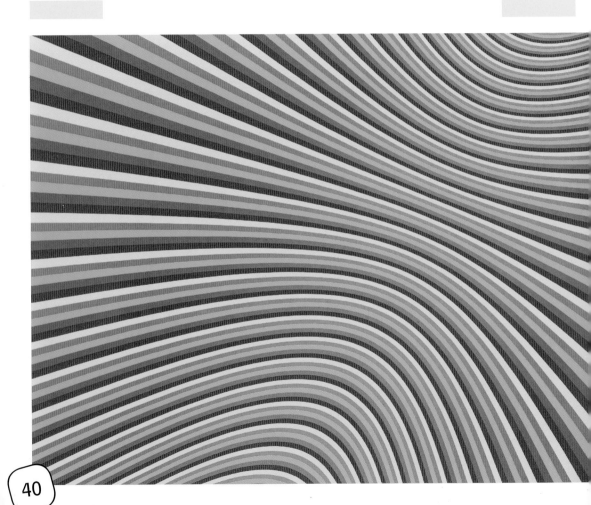

Are these lines bending inwards or outwards? When you stare at the point where they bend, can you see a shimmering effect?

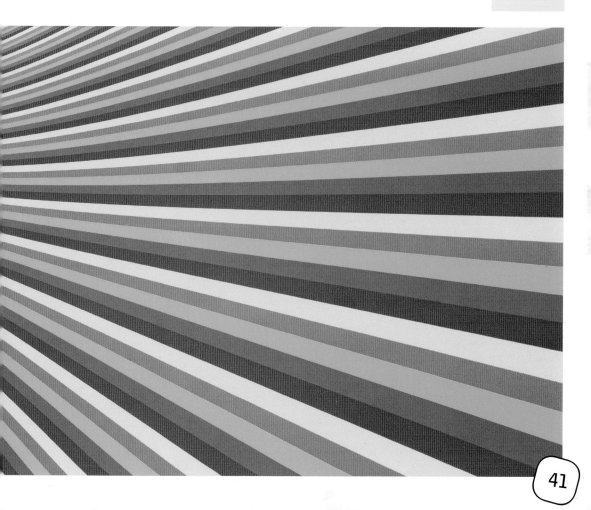

CRACKED?

Your brain thinks it knows what a building looks like, and persistently 'corrects' your eye when it tells you that this construction is impossible!

WHEELS WITHIN WHEELS

How many different circles of movement can you see at once? Usually just the outer two circles seem to move, but can you spot the inner ones moving?

WINDOW OR WHAT?

You've probably guessed this isn't a real window. But what is it? The answer is below.

It's a sundial.

MERGED 'Z'S

Do you see a light grey forwards 'Z'
or a black backwards one?

TWISTING TEST

How long can you stare at the spinning circle without having to blink? Time yourself!

BALANCING ACT

Who do you think will fall off first?

MANGLED MECHANISM

Not only would these wheels never turn in real life,
but you could never build them in the first place.

AFTERIMAGES

Stare at the white dot for 30 seconds, then close your eyes. What do you see?

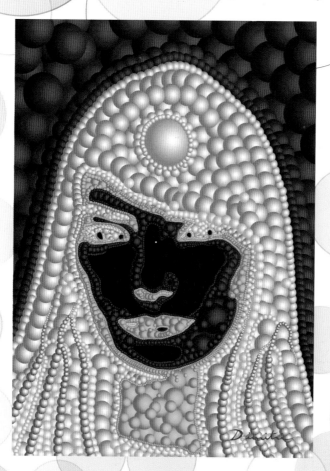

These afterimage portraits by Dimitri Parant work by overstimulating some cells in the eye and understimulating others.

LASER LIGHTS

This moving illusion consists of the pattern made by a reflected laser beam.

WINK AT ME

If you look at this illusion with one eye instead of both, it may move less or not at all. This is because with only one eye in play your brain is receiving less contradictory information.

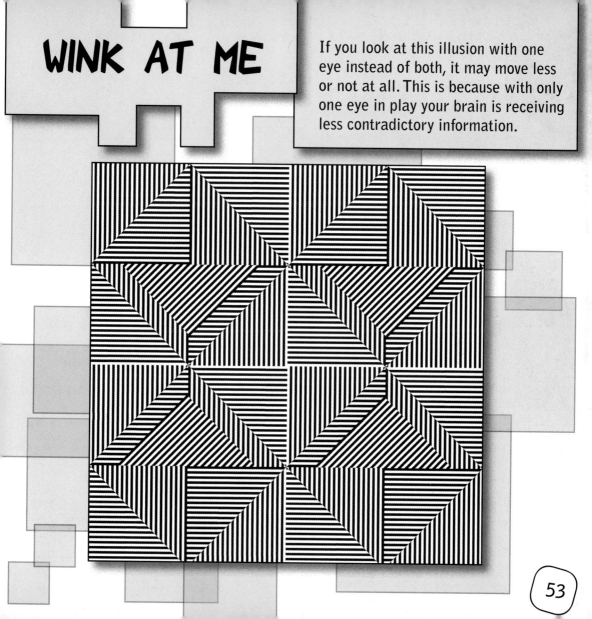

ETERNITY RING

This simple illusion has no beginning and no end,
but it looks as if you could wear it on your finger.

SPINNING TUNNEL

The 'V's seem to circle endlessly. But do the ones on the red streak seem to move less than the others?

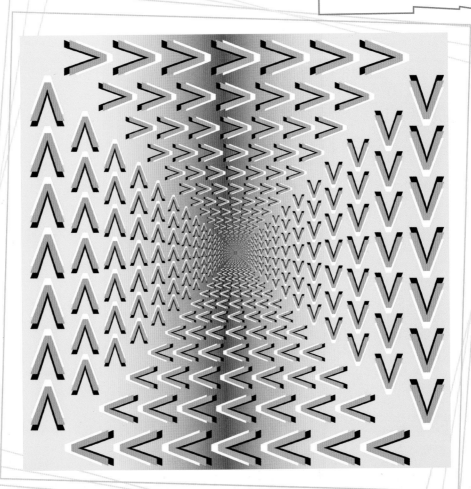

PENGUIN PLAYGROUND

This construction creates an 'impossible reality'.

PLUMBING THE HEIGHTS

This is not actually an optical illusion, but a real sculpture in Ypres, Belgium.

BURSTING BULGE

This illusion is a more protruding version of the Bogus Bulge on page 13.

CUBE ACCUMULATION

In this kind of image, each cube looks entirely realistic on its own – but they add up to something much less likely.

WHO ARE WE?

The princess and her grumpy stepmother... or the other way around?

TRY THIS ONE AT HOME!

You might not have a bird bath the size of the one outside this Bavarian castle, but why not hold a dish in front of your house so that the house 'sits' on it?

ELECTRIC AVENUE

If you stand in the right place, this piece of street art in Poland looks three-dimensional.

STRETCHING CREDIBILITY

This sculpture at Cairo airport is possible because the 'rocks' are actually made of a paper-mache-like material.

OLD OR YOUNG?

This optical illusion was printed on a German postcard in 1888, but may have been known before that.

CALM CENTRE?

By focusing on the absolute centre, can you make this pulsing image stay still?

STRAIGHTEN ME OUT

If you removed two cubes from this figure, it would cease to be an illusion. Can you work out which ones they are?

The two that form a bar across the middle of the figure.

WIGGIN OUT!

Cyclist Bradley Wiggins comes face to face with jungle street art created by Kurt Wenner.

TRY THIS ONE AT HOME!

Who do you want to step on?
Make sure they get a turn at stepping on you too!

HANGING AROUND

Artist Leandro Erlich painted a housefront on the ground and hung a huge mirror above it so people could lie down and see themselves 'suspended' from the walls!

PORT CUT

Did this homeowner chop through their wall
to provide quick access to the beach?

SEWER SURPRISE

Turtles erupt from a fake sewer in this street art by 3D Joe and Max.

TRY THIS ONE AT HOME!

You could set up this shot in your local park. Or, if you live in a flat with a balcony, you could replace the balcony bottom with your arm!

SQUIRMING CIRCLE

Can you count the 'V's in the centre circle, or do they squirm too much? The total is below.

There are 59 'V's in the centre circle.

SUSPENSION OF DISBELIEF

The 'natural' way the light is depicted here fools the eye into thinking this image should work like a real shelf.

SHIFTING SANDS

Do you see a desert scene, a dog or a face? Or all three?

PULSATING BLACK HOLE

The blue lozenges rush to be swallowed up, but never actually get there.

TRY THIS ONE AT HOME!

Is anyone in your family annoyingly tall? Set up this photo to cut them down to size!

SPIDER SENSE

This amazing art is drawn on a flat surface but looks like a deep canyon between buildings when viewed from the right spot.

81

MARVELLOUS MARBLE

This marble spins without needing to be pushed!

WATER BOGGLER

This is a three-dimensional rendering of a famous piece by artist Maurits Escher, who specialised in images of impossible constructions.

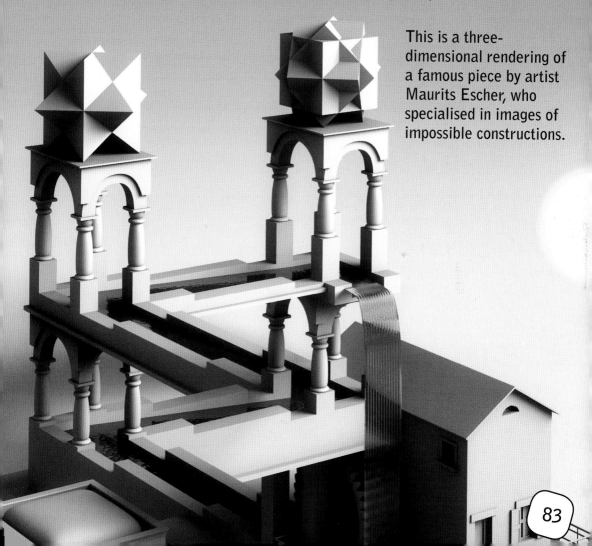

THE BIG CITY

A model city? No, this is a real suburb of Istanbul, captured with tilt-shift photography, which creates a blur around the edge of an image and sharpens the centre.

1 2 3 4 5 6 7 8 9 10 11 12 13 14

ENDLESS CLIMB

Can you make these impossible stairs out of paper?
Then, can you take a photo at an angle that makes it look real?

MAGIC MOSAIC

This two-dimensional image seems to move like the beads in a kaleidoscope. (If you don't know what that is, ask your parents!)

THE PARROWDOX

Try copying this drawing. First do the lines, and then the shading. Can you see how the shading strengthens the three-dimensional effect?

UNDULATING PAPER

This illusion uses the bulge effect seen on pages 13 and 59 to create an effect of multiple undulations, or waves.

BREAKING BOUNDS

Because we are so used to seeing pictures within frames, a picture that spills over looks like a real object. Here the tiger, the frame and the shadow are all painted.

GHOST IMAGES

These negatives of Clark Cable and Greta Garbo work similarly to the afterimages on pages 49 to 51. Stare at the four white dots for 30 seconds, then shut your eyes.

ARROW WRAP

Is the green arrow bent or straight?

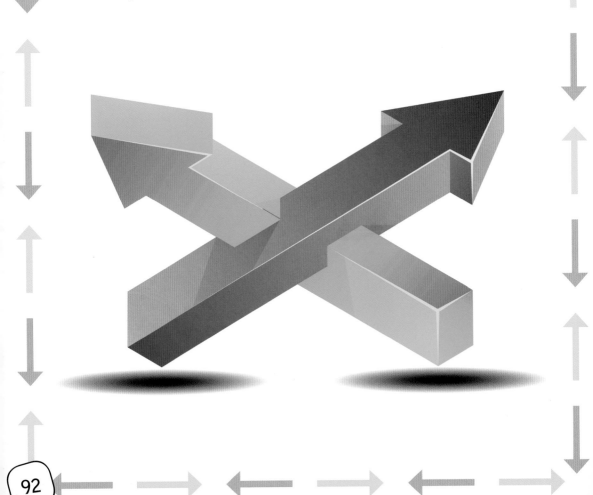